DRAMA CLUB

Activity Book & Glossary

Theater Edition

AGES 8–14

By Avery Clyde

Actor Food Publishing

FREE VIDEO BONUS!

JOIN THE CAST!

FOLLOW US ON AMAZON

ACTOR FOOD

WELCOME to DRAMA CLUB!

Hello young creatives! Thanks for purchasing my first ever book!! OMG I'm so excited! With 30+ years of experience in the industry (I've been an actor since I was in school like you!!) it will be hard to contain myself in a activity book but I wanted to start at the beginning. For young creatives the first step is to just be curious and play.

Let your imagination wander while getting familiar with a life in the arts. High impact journal prompts like "How do you know if you're an actor?", actor hacks, word searches, crossword puzzles, a blocking decoder and a glossary of over 50 theater terms. A fun, mindful space of self expression...and imagination.

MORE MORE MORE: QR CODE
Once you receive your book; scan the code and there's a FREE VIDEO workshop from me! I'll walk through all the key terms on a real stage.

I love what I do and I'm excited to share it with you at any age.
Actor Food was created to feed the starving artist. The creative arts have been such a savior to me and my family. The space of freedom and love and just being seen. To me the arts aren't extra curricular but essential to the growth and balanced well being of our kids. I hope you'll join me again and again to nurture that together.

Thank you so much for your purchase and support of
ACTOR FOOD: Drama Club Activity Book & Glossary (Theater Edition)
My cast of Clydes are so grateful.
Stay curious
xo Avery

...to feed the starving artist

Artist Oath

I promise to play.
I promise to respect myself,
the words and the cast and crew.
I promise to always be curious.

This book belongs to:

Signature:________________________
Date:___________________________

Drama Club Cast

"Cast" intros by Lushi

JAMES: He got cast as "Prince" (Prince Charming). It's his first play and mom says you get nervous with your lines at first. Mostly James is on the tennis court with his dad. He dresses really nice (like his clothes have no wrinkles), maybe he'll be a Ben Shelton or Frances Tiafoe, someday!

GLORIA: Wow, she's been an actress since she was 5! She's playing the part of "Cindy" (Cinderella). She helps James with his lines alot & I think she's really pretty and brave. She'd be a great director someday.

VIOLA: This is my mom and the director of "Slippers" this season's play at school. She's pretty cool. She's the tech director, costume designer, prop master, well...a lot of stuff at drama club. But I'm pretty sure she loves every second!

PARKER: is our youngest crew member, her favorite color is pink, she also loves power tools and running lights. She runs the follow spot and also helps mom with sound too.

CORNDOG: He'll play Cindy's cat in "Slippers". He always yells "I'm the King of the DRAMA GEEKS!" My mom says there's a kid like that in every club.... he's funny and magically knows lots of random stuff.

LUSHI: That's me. I'm the Fairy GodMother! Can't believe mom cast me! I'm just excited to get out there but Gloria makes James say his lines word perfect, so I wait alot. If only these fairy wings really worked.

CLYDE: He's a high school kid. He must really love theater too cuz he's always here. Mom says he basically runs the tech crew and is the stage manager. We call him Cuke, cuz he's so calm. LOL. Oh and he is WAY TALL, like he makes chairs look small.

OPENING NIGHT IS SOON!!

Left: These are Japanese Kabuki theater masks: known for their exaggerated faces, to portray a variety of characters.

Viola's Director's Note: Hey creative kids, our drama club is working toward Opening Night. Our play is inspired by Cinderella but in this version, Cindy runs away with Prince and they launch: CPC Slippers, the most "Charming" shoe company.

Cold Reading - a performance of text or music with no time to prepare.

SHOWTIME
FAIRY GODMOTHER
1

Headshot - photo business cards for performers...mostly of their head. (Put your headshot in the frame. If you don't have a headshot, put a family photo or just draw one of yourself and write your first and last name on the line! Play. Play. Play.)

CAST

Resume - a list of past acting work and training, professionally typed. Resumes can be digital or printed and cut to 8x10 then stapled to the back of your headshot.

1
LUSHI
GLORIA
ESIAS

Audition - a short performance to show someone's talent.
Sides - a few pages from 1 or more scenes, given by the casting director before auditions.
Script - written words of a play, movie or broadcast.Created to perform.

SHOWTI

Callbacks - an invitation to return for a second audition or interview.
Casting - the assigning of parts in a production to an actor or actors.

Warm Up - warming up your body and vocal cords for any performance. It is different for every performer but I've used the same physical and vocal warm up for years.
Depending on the character you might take time to just get into character (focus on it) and shake off the day.

1
BIG
BODY
LITTLE
BODY
1
BIG
BODY

In 1 word: Acting & theater make me feel:

Close your eyes.
Imagine you're a professional actor or artist.
Write or draw what you see.

Audition

Q	U	K	V	I	A	W	I	W	M	E	M	O	R	I	Z	E	Q
Y	N	D	I	R	E	C	T	O	R	N	Y	T	C	R	E	N	I
N	O	W	A	Y	H	F	F	Q	X	K	D	T	E	H	V	W	H
I	M	P	R	O	V	I	S	A	T	I	O	N	U	G	O	E	M
R	C	O	H	Y	G	C	J	I	W	H	T	Z	E	U	Y	A	Y
C	R	U	B	F	O	T	I	Q	S	R	P	O	K	P	A	U	R
S	O	K	E	S	Q	W	K	D	A	U	C	L	T	U	F	D	Q
P	S	L	T	X	O	Y	A	P	M	R	K	N	E	Z	J	I	X
H	S	E	D	G	C	E	E	R	O	N	A	E	V	A	G	T	J
O	W	S	W	R	H	N	A	O	S	G	P	S	Y	Y	D	I	S
L	R	Z	U	O	E	W	R	E	H	E	A	R	S	A	L	O	E
C	E	A	B	C	C	A	D	E	F	T	B	P	P	D	F	N	W
M	S	J	S	D	E	I	D	Q	X	P	N	S	J	P	M	C	R
E	U	Y	F	Z	S	D	Z	I	L	I	N	E	S	H	J	V	W
U	M	P	A	T	C	V	M	O	N	O	L	O	G	U	E	Q	C
I	E	H	U	L	B	K	R	H	T	G	B	T	G	O	H	Q	E
A	P	W	S	T	N	D	W	T	L	K	I	S	B	O	X	F	G
Z	X	V	J	E	S	S	R	H	V	G	O	C	X	L	I	Q	B

AUDITION
CUE
IMPROVISATION
MEMORIZE
RESUME
WARMUP

COLD READING
DIRECTOR
LEAD
MONOLOGUE
SCENE PARTNER

CROSS
HEADSHOT
LINES
REHEARSAL
SIDES

5W's: Quick "Actor's Process" for any scene. Just ask yourself these questions about the scene and be as detailed as you can. **W**ho, **W**hat, **W**here, **W**hen and **W**hy. Who's in the scene? What do they want? Where are they? When is it? and Why?

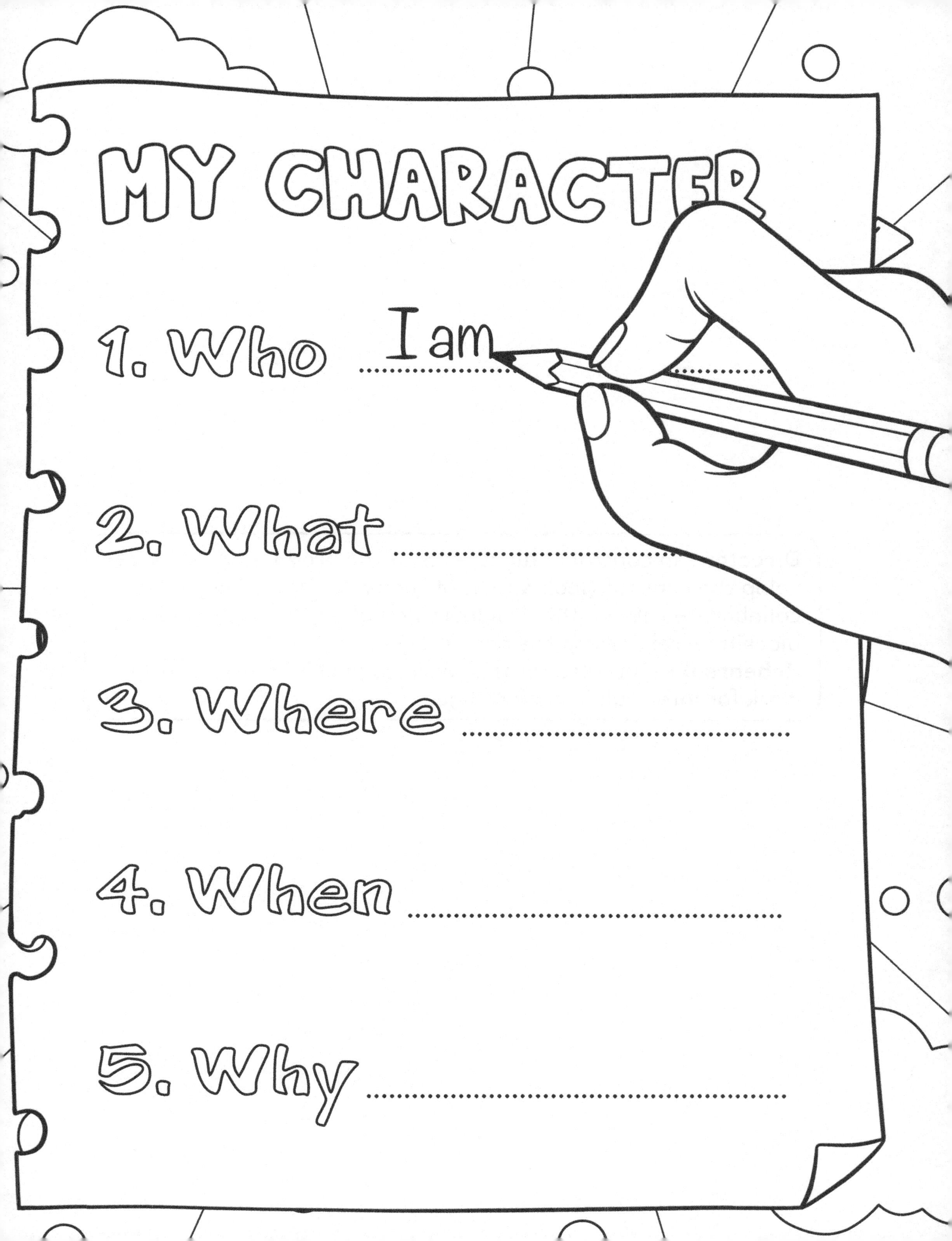
MY CHARACTER
1. Who I am
2. What
3. Where
4. When
5. Why

Director - in control of all aspects of the production. They develop the concept (look & feel) of the production. They lead & collaborate with all the designers and of course they manage blocking & rehearsing the actors.
Rehearsal - a practice or trial performance of a play or other work for later public performance.

Lead - the main protagonist. In other words the character that the problem or challenge of the play seems to center around.
Lines - the words of dialogue said by an actor from a play or script.
Actor hack - playwrights about to premiere a new play often change: lines, pages or scenes with no notice. With new works use a paper script & a pencil only for the easiest rehearsal process.

Monologue - a long speech by one actor in a play or movie.
Cue - when a certain line or action should begin. Some say it comes from the Latin word quando, shortened to "q" (say q out loud) meaning "when".

Blocking - the location and movement of actors on stage.
Cross-X - moving from one part of the stage to another. Marked with an "X"in your script.
Improvisation - a form of performance or rehearsal in which the plot,characters and dialogue of a game, scene or story are made up in the moment.

X = CROSS
CROSS DOWNSTAGE
RIGHT

Backstage - area where actors wait till it's their entrance to go on stage. The "behind the scenes" area of any production.
Stage Curtains - heavy dark/black curtains hung around the stage to shape the playing areas for the actors and to block or "mask" the backstage from the audience.

Upstage/Downstage : **US/DS** - up stage is the back of the stage farthest from the audience. Downstage is closest to the audience. During Shakespeare's time, actors played on a **raked stage** (a stage higher in the back than the front) so the folks in the pit (standing on the ground in front of the stage.) could see. So all directions are from standing on the stage, Center Center. On your script you'd write US for upstage and DS for downstage.

UPSTAGE
DOWNSTAGE

Stage Left/Stage Right : SL/SR - Stand center center CC & look at the audience. SL is to your left and SR is to your right.

STAGE
RIGHT
(SR)
STAGE
LEFT
(SL)

Wings - the areas just off stage left or stage right, not seen by the audience.
Off stage - a position backstage or in the wings as to not be seen by the audience.

Center Stage : CS - the central and prominent position on stage. Central playing area. Center Center CC is smack dab in the middle and considered the most powerful spot on stage.

Proscenium - the frame or arch separating the stage from the house/auditorium, through it we view the action of the play often referred to as the fourth wall.

Set - a created stage space where the action of a performance takes place. Scenery, furniture and the overall look of the stage is the job of the set designer.

Flat - a lightweight wood frame, covered with canvas or plywood. Flats are easy to move as walls, arranged to create a backdrop for a stage set.

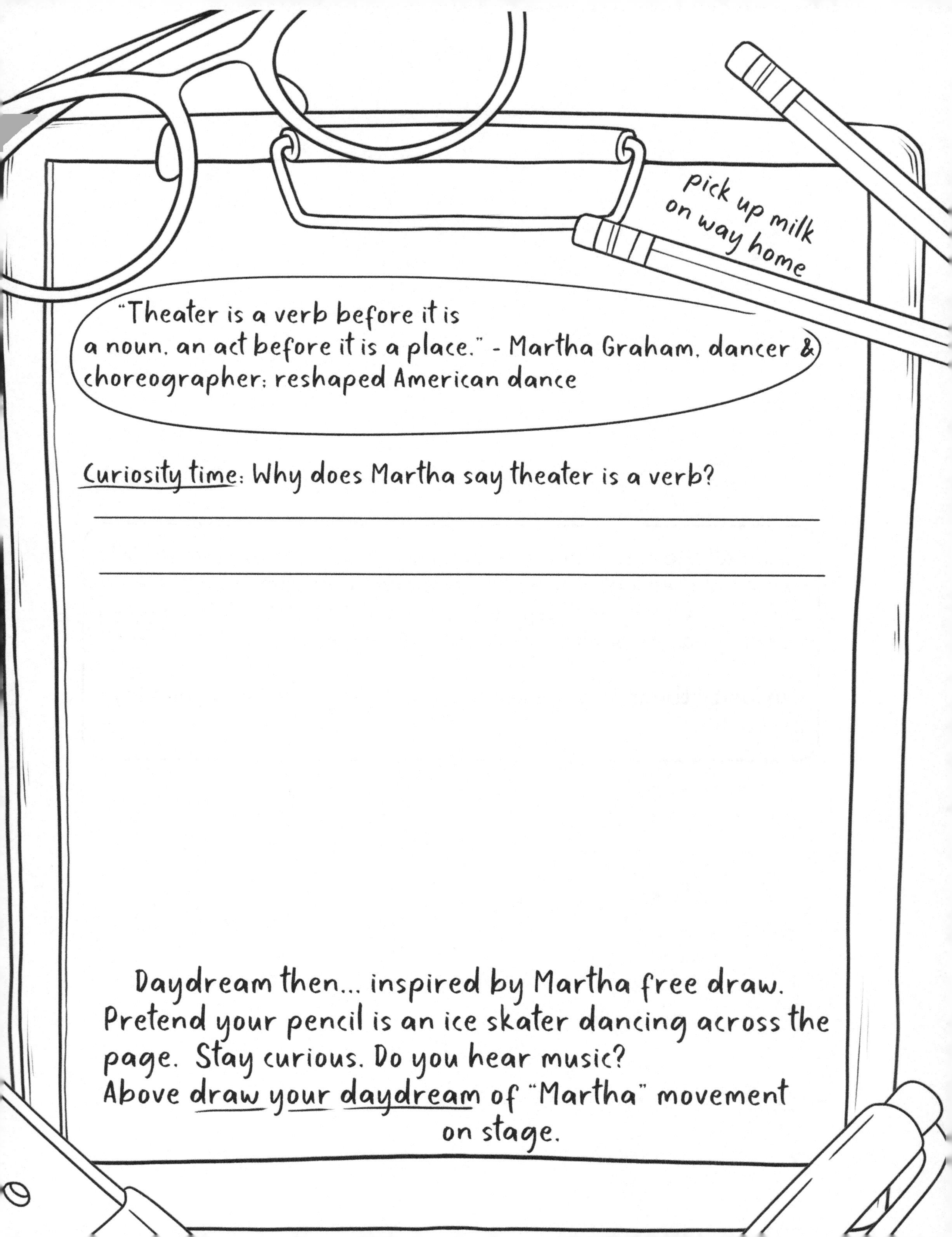
pick up milk
on way home
"Theater is a verb before it is
a noun, an act before it is a place." - Martha Graham, dancer &
choreographer; reshaped American dance
Curiosity time: Why does Martha say theater is a verb?
Daydream then... inspired by Martha free draw.
Pretend your pencil is an ice skater dancing across the
page. Stay curious. Do you hear music?
Above draw your daydream of "Martha" movement
on stage.

...And all the men and women merely players; they have their exits and their entrances; and one man in his time plays many parts..." William Shakespeare's, 'As You Like It'. Widely known as the greatest playwright of the English language.

Curiosity time: Billy Shakes might ask, what roles do you play in real life?

FIRST PLAY
I EVER SAW. DATE:
FIRST TIME
IN FRONT OF AN
AUDIENCE. DATE:
FIRST WORDS
I EVERY SAID ON A
STAGE. DATE:
PERFORMING FOR YOUR
FAMILY ON THE FRONT
PORCH TOTALLY COUNTS!
ALL THE WORLD'S A
STAGE, RIGHT?!

Rehearsal

G	P	R	B	Y	H	N	N	R	Y	S	R	M	R	K	V	J	E
C	V	C	Q	I	W	N	T	M	P	Y	C	H	X	X	S	F	N
R	Z	S	W	W	Z	P	Z	B	L	O	C	K	I	N	G	F	X
O	C	E	N	T	E	R	C	E	N	T	E	R	I	Z	E	O	Y
S	N	T	O	D	P	A	G	S	L	G	N	A	F	R	R	F	X
S	Y	W	N	S	Y	A	G	S	A	C	T	Q	D	L	M	F	S
V	E	U	D	M	T	N	V	T	Y	R	E	X	O	E	A	S	C
E	O	Z	B	S	I	E	S	U	U	G	R	O	G	U	Q	T	E
J	V	O	N	W	S	K	S	C	A	G	S	A	M	T	J	A	N
C	R	W	S	U	C	S	E	T	Y	O	T	P	Q	B	F	G	E
D	O	P	O	A	A	G	S	M	A	S	A	S	O	N	V	E	R
D	I	P	B	X	A	P	U	L	D	G	G	A	M	Y	X	L	Y
U	E	Y	O	T	U	H	S	E	T	D	E	S	I	G	N	E	R
N	J	B	S	Y	K	K	K	C	M	I	J	R	M	Q	M	F	E
Z	E	W	W	S	G	A	L	D	K	A	L	G	I	Q	I	T	L
S	W	U	Y	P	R	O	S	C	E	N	I	U	M	G	G	S	V
F	T	L	A	M	L	O	C	V	I	E	R	G	Y	T	H	P	S
A	O	N	K	H	L	H	C	P	G	N	S	C	R	I	P	T	X

BACKSTAGE
RAKED STAGE
WINGS
OFFSTAGE
STAGE RIGHT
PROSCENIUM
UPSTAGE

CENTERSTAGE
SET
BLOCKING
SCENERY
CENTER CENTER
SCRIPT

FLAT
STAGE LEFT
CROSS
SET DESIGNER
DOWNSTAGE
STAGE CURTAINS

Break a leg!

Across

1. A midday performance traditionally at 2pm.
4. Auditorium or audience. "We had a good ____tonight." aka a good audience. In front of the stage curtain.
5. After rehearsal, the director or stage manager's report to the cast & crew of what worked and what didnt.
9. Opening through closing of any 1 show or event.

Down

2. 1–5 major sections within a play. A short play is called a 1 ___ play.
3. A moment in the theater when the lights on stage are suddenly turned off.
6. A classic Greek ________was a group of actors who commented on the main action through words, song or dance
7. A phrase that means "good luck" in the theater. It's true orign is unknown.
8. An ______ is an actor who learns the lines, blocking and choreography, of 1 of more characters in a play, They step in and perform should a cast member become unavailable

Tech Rehearsal - a rehearsal focused on just the technical elements. (Lights, sounds, props, costumes and any special effects.) Actors are present but the focus is on the technical elements. (See DRAMA CLUB Activity Book-Theater Edition TEENS & Young professionals for all the all the different kinds of techs during a production).
Props - any object used on stage or screen by an actor.
Costumes - clothing used by a performer on stage and picked out or created by a costume designer.

Dressing rooms - a room in the theater where performers prepare to go on stage and put on their costumes and makeup.
Dress Rehearsal - usually within the last 1-2 weeks of rehearsal before opening. In this rehearsal actors wear their costumes, use their props and rehearse with all the lights, sounds and tech. The real deal without an audience.

Stage manager - handles all communication with the cast and crew; acts as a right hand to the director; oversees sets, props, lights, and sound; and calls all technical cues (different lights & sound etc) during a performance.

STAGE
MANAGE

Opening Night - a production is performed in front of an audience for the first time.
Playwright - writers who specialize in telling stories for the stage. If it's a new play the playwright might be in the audience on opening night!

Green Room - functions as a waiting room, before, during and after a performance; when actors are not engaged on stage.

06:00 PM
SPORT

TICKETS
LIPPERS
NOW
SHOWING

Closing - the final performance of a show. As they say in the movie's that's a wrap! Happy Closing!

CPC SLIPPERS
CPC
CPC
1

Cast party - a party for the cast and crew involved in a production where they can relax and celebrate after a closing show.

1

Strike - reset of the stage; removal of sets, props, costumes, lights and sound equipment.

BE. DO. HAVE.
1
“I’m being an artist in my mind. I’m doing the actions artists do. I have the proof I’m an actor”

Showtime

Y	N	F	P	P	L	A	Y	W	R	I	G	H	T	C	D	A	S	Z
I	O	P	E	N	I	N	G	N	I	G	H	T	U	K	B	I	S	J
T	U	T	G	D	I	A	N	Y	S	O	Z	H	D	B	X	C	C	H
A	U	L	D	H	X	C	O	S	T	U	M	E	S	B	C	W	A	S
Z	C	B	Z	R	K	U	F	X	A	A	X	P	Z	O	D	V	M	B
D	E	O	K	C	E	W	R	S	G	N	R	I	W	X	R	C	Q	Z
L	C	O	F	J	A	S	Z	C	E	P	Z	N	O	O	E	B	A	O
D	Q	Z	N	I	J	S	S	X	M	F	P	V	W	F	S	J	D	V
G	H	W	N	D	A	C	T	I	A	T	X	M	D	F	S	J	G	C
J	Q	Q	E	K	X	W	T	P	N	N	W	C	M	I	R	W	P	L
S	H	M	O	W	D	R	X	V	A	G	D	Q	E	C	E	T	I	O
D	O	Q	G	N	I	J	H	V	G	R	R	D	Q	E	H	M	N	S
G	Y	S	V	S	Z	H	O	P	E	P	T	O	C	O	E	Z	C	I
N	P	C	B	M	H	O	F	L	R	T	R	Y	O	R	A	K	D	N
K	I	O	Y	N	U	K	K	V	O	R	I	O	C	M	R	Q	L	G
D	P	D	V	G	R	E	E	N	R	O	O	M	P	K	S	C	U	I
E	G	K	H	T	U	I	H	Y	P	X	X	G	U	S	A	H	C	S
V	O	N	T	E	C	H	R	E	H	E	A	R	S	A	L	K	G	Y
R	O	Z	C	T	E	Z	W	X	D	B	D	Y	W	M	K	Q	T	X

BOX OFFICE
PROPS
OPENING NIGHT
DRESS REHEARSAL
COSTUMES
CAST PARTY
STAGE MANAGER
PLAYWRIGHT
GREEN ROOM
DRESSING ROOMS
CLOSING
TECH REHEARSAL

"Being an artist you have to abandon the notion of things making sense", María Irene Fornés, Cuban American playwright known for "Fefu and her friends."

ACTOR HACK: When memorizing lines, walk around the block. The activity and movement distracts you like on stage. If someone passes and can't tell you're rehearsing lines. SCORE!

"If you don't see a clear path for what you want, sometimes you have to make it yourself." Mindy Kaling Writer, Producer, Actor "The Mindy Project"

Character Research - PARKER

Draw to complete Parker's dooble page like you think she would.

BLOCKING DECODER

Click the QR code on page 1 to see the decoder come to life!

Using a pencil actors write these codes in their script; to remember their blocking (stage movement).

A stage is a grid; like a game of tic–tac–toe.

Upstage Right	Upstage Center	Upstage Left
Center Stage Right	Center Stage Center	Center Stage Left
Downstage Right	Downstage Center	Downstage Left

X = Cross Example: XDSR = Cross Downstage Right

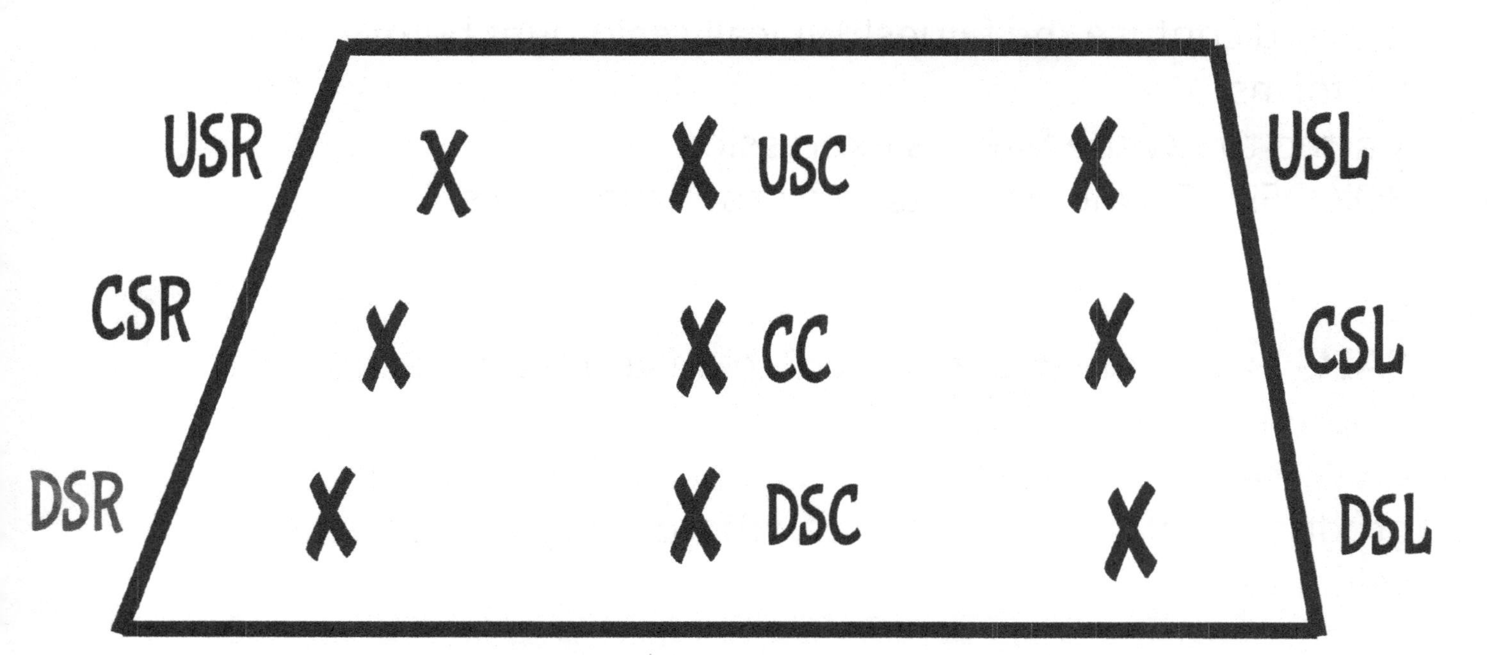

GLOSSARY
...everyone starts here.

A

ACT - 1-5 big sections within a play. Each act is made up of scenes. A short play is called a 1 Act Play.
AUDITION- a short performance to show someone's talent and training.

B

BACKSTAGE- area where actors wait for their cue to enter. The "behind the scenes" area of any show.
BLACK OUT- a moment in the theater when the lights on stage are suddenly turned off.
BLOCKING - the "traffic pattern" or movements of actors on stage. Actors write their blocking in their scripts. Actor hack: Actors only use pencil to write blocking down, as it often changes.
BREAK A LEG- In the theater saying "good luck" is actually considered bad luck. Rumor has it that theater ghosts and fairies like to give the opposite: "Bad Luck!" So instead we say, "break a leg" and confuse the fairies! Typically said right before an actor performs. Many theories but no one is certain how exactly we started to say the famous expression..
BOX OFFICE- where tickets to a production are sold.

C

CALL- exact time you're "called" to be at the theater, ready to start a performance or rehearsal.
CAST PARTY- a party for the cast and crew involved in a production after a show closes, where everyone can relax and celebrate.

CENTER STAGE-CS the central and prominent position on stage. Central playing area when facing the audience
CHORUS-in a drama or musical, those who perform vocally in a group versus solo. A classic Greek Chorus was a group of actors who commented on the main action through words, song or dance giving extra clues to the audience.
CLOSING-the final performance of a show.
COLD READING-a performance of text or music with no preparation.
COSTUMES-clothing used by a performer on stage and chosen or created by a costume designer.
COVER/UNDERSTUDY/SWING-an actor who learns the lines, blocking and choreography of 1 or more characters. If an actor in the cast can't perform (even during a show) the swing or understudy will step in. Covering for a character is a great opportunity, challenge and entry point for new actors.

CROSS- X moving from one part of the stage to another. Marked with an "X" in your script.
CUE-when a certain line or action should begin. Some say it comes from the Latin word quando, shortened to "q" (say q out loud) meaning "when".

D
DIRECTOR -In control of all aspects of the production. They develop the concept of the production,briefs the designer and lighting designer, plots the actor's moves, rehearses the actors, etc.

DOWN STAGE is the front of the stage closest to the audience. (See Up Stage for complete description)
DRESS REHEARSAL -usually within the last 1-2 weeks of rehearsal before opening. In this rehearsal actors wear their costumes, use their props and rehearse with all the lights, sounds and tech. The real deal without an audience.
DRESSING ROOMS -a room in the theater where performers prepare to go on stage and put on their costumes and makeup.

F

FLAT-a lightweight wood frame, covered with canvas or plywood. Flats are easy to move as walls, arranged to create a backdrop for a stage set.

G

GREEN ROOM-functions as a waiting room, before, during and after a performance; when actors are not engaged on stage.

H

HEADSHOT 8x10 photo business cards for performers...mostly of their head.
HOUSE-used to mean the auditorium or the audience it's anything on the audience side of the curtain. "We had a good house tonight." aka we had a good audience. Also know as FOH or front of house.

I

IMPROV-a form of performance or rehearsal in which the plot, characters and dialogue of a game, scene or story are made up in the moment.

L

LINES-the words of dialogue said by actor from a play or script.

LEAD-the main protagonist. In other words the character that the problem or challenge of the play seems to center around.

M

MATINEE a midday performance traditionally at 2pm.

MONOLOGUE a long speech by one actor in a play or movie, or as part of a theatrical or broadcast program.

N

NOTES Director and/or stage manager feedback given after rehearsal. They tell the cast and crew what worked and what needs to be adjusted before the next rehearsal or performance. (set, costumes, lights, sound, blocking, lines, props etc.)

O

OFF STAGE a position backstage or in the wings; as to not be seen by the audience.

P

PROSCENIUM the frame or arch separating the stage from the house/auditorium, through it we view the action of the play.

R

RAKED STAGE a stage higher in the back(US) than the front(DS). In Shakespeare's time it helped those standing and watching from the pit (the cheap seats) see better. So all stage directions are from standing on the stage, Center Center as if it was a raked stage.

REHEARSAL a practice or trial performance of a play or other work for later public performance.

RESUME a list of past acting work and training, professionally typed. Resumes can be digital or printed and cut to 8x10 then stapled to the back of your headshot.

RUN Opening through closing of any 1 show or event.

S

SCENE PARTNER- the other actor or actors with you in any 1 scene.

SET a created stage space where the action of a performance takes place. Scenery, furniture and the overall look of the stage is the job of the set designer.
SCRIPT written text of a play, movie or broadcast, intended for performance
SIDES traditionally a few pages from 1+ scenes of the script, given by the casting director before auditions.
STAGE CURTAINS heavy dark curtains hung around the stage to shape the playing area. They're also used to block or "mask" the backstage from the audience.
STAGE LEFT standing CC looking at the audience. SL is to your left and marked SL when writing down your blocking in your script.
STAGE MANAGER -handles all communication with the cast and crew; acts as a right hand to the director; oversees sets, props, lights, and sound; and calls all technical cues (lights & sounds etc that occur during a show) during a performance.
STAGE RIGHT standing CC looking at the audience. Stage Right is to your right and marked SR when writing down your blocking in your script.
SWING/UNDERSTUDY/COVER an actor who learns the lines, blocking and choreography of 1 or more characters. If an actor in the cast can't perform (even during a show) the swing or understudy will step in. Covering for a character is a great opportunity and entry point for new actors, while being one of the most challenging jobs on stage.

O

OPENING NIGHT -a production is performed in front of an audience officially for the first time.

P

PLAYWRIGHT-writers who specialize in telling stories for the stage. If it's a new play the playwright is usually in the audience on opening night!
PROPS-any object used on stage or screen by an actor.

T

TECH REHEARSAL-a rehearsal focused on just the technical elements. (Lights, sounds, props, costumes and any special effects.) Actors are present but the focus is on the technical elements.

U

UPSTAGE/DOWNSTAGE -US/DS Up stage is the back of the stage farthest from the audience. Down stage is closest to the audience. On your script you'd write US for upstage and DS for downstage.

W

W's A simple way to figure out a character or role. Just ask yourself these questions about the script and be as detailed as you can. Who, What, Where, When and Why. Who's in the scene? What do they want? Where are they? When is it ? Why are you there.

WARM UP Warming up your body and vocal cords for any performance. It different for every performer but I've used the same physical and vocal warm up for years. Depending on the character you might take time to just get into character and let the day go.
WINGS-the areas just off stage left or stage right, not seen by the audience.

Audition Key

Q	U	K	V	I	A	W	I	W	M	E	M	O	R	I	Z	E	Q
Y	N	D	I	R	E	C	T	O	R	N	Y	T	C	R	E	N	I
N	O	W	A	Y	H	F	F	Q	X	K	D	T	E	H	V	W	H
I	M	P	R	O	V	I	S	A	T	I	O	N	U	G	O	E	M
R	C	O	H	Y	G	C	J	I	W	H	T	Z	E	U	Y	A	Y
C	R	U	B	F	O	T	I	Q	S	R	P	O	K	P	A	U	R
S	O	K	E	S	Q	W	K	D	A	U	C	L	T	U	F	D	Q
P	S	L	T	X	O	Y	A	P	M	R	K	N	E	Z	J	I	X
H	S	E	D	G	C	E	E	R	O	N	A	E	V	A	G	T	J
O	W	S	W	R	H	N	A	O	S	G	P	S	Y	Y	D	I	S
L	R	Z	U	O	E	W	R	E	H	E	A	R	S	A	L	O	E
C	E	A	B	C	C	A	D	E	F	T	B	P	P	D	F	N	W
M	S	J	S	D	E	I	D	Q	X	P	N	S	J	P	M	C	R
E	U	Y	F	Z	S	D	Z	I	L	I	N	E	S	H	J	V	W
U	M	P	A	T	C	V	M	O	N	O	L	O	G	U	E	Q	C
I	E	H	U	L	B	K	R	H	T	G	B	T	G	O	H	Q	E
A	P	W	S	T	N	D	W	T	L	K	I	S	B	O	X	F	G
Z	X	V	J	E	S	S	R	H	V	G	O	C	X	L	I	Q	B

Rehearsal Key

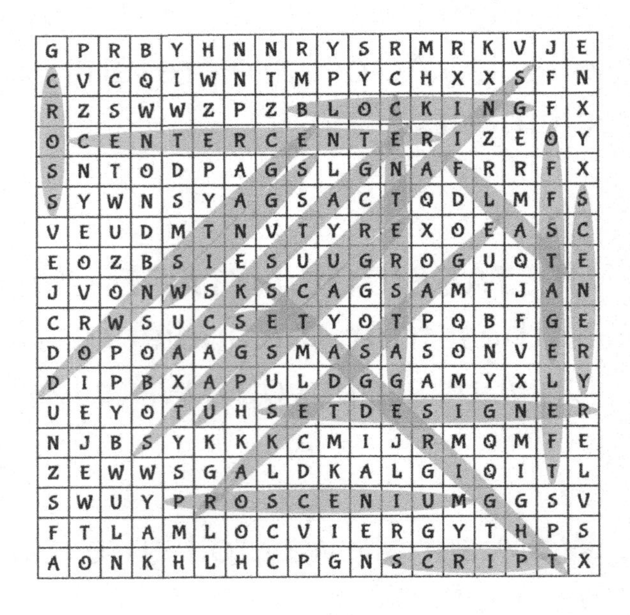

Showtime Key

Y	N	F	P	P	L	A	Y	W	R	I	G	H	T	C	D	A	S	Z
I	O	P	E	N	I	N	G	N	I	G	H	T	U	K	B	I	S	J
T	U	T	G	D	I	A	N	Y	S	O	Z	H	D	B	X	C	C	H
A	U	L	D	H	X	C	O	S	T	U	M	E	S	B	C	W	A	S
Z	C	B	Z	R	K	U	F	X	A	A	X	P	Z	O	D	V	M	B
D	E	O	K	C	E	W	R	S	G	N	R	I	W	X	R	C	Q	Z
L	C	O	F	J	A	S	Z	C	E	P	Z	N	O	O	E	B	A	O
D	Q	Z	N	I	J	S	S	X	M	F	P	V	W	F	S	J	D	V
G	H	W	N	D	A	C	T	I	A	T	X	M	D	F	S	J	G	C
J	Q	Q	E	K	X	W	T	P	N	N	W	C	M	I	R	W	P	L
S	H	M	O	W	D	R	X	V	A	G	D	Q	E	C	E	T	I	O
D	O	Q	G	N	I	J	H	V	G	R	R	D	Q	E	H	M	N	S
G	Y	S	V	S	Z	H	O	P	E	P	T	O	C	O	E	Z	C	I
N	P	C	B	M	H	O	F	L	R	T	R	Y	O	R	A	K	D	N
K	I	O	Y	N	U	K	K	V	O	R	I	O	C	M	R	Q	L	G
D	P	D	V	G	R	E	E	N	R	O	O	M	P	K	S	C	U	I
E	G	K	H	T	U	I	H	Y	P	X	X	G	U	S	A	H	C	S
V	O	N	T	E	C	H	R	E	H	E	A	R	S	A	L	K	G	Y
R	O	Z	C	T	E	Z	W	X	D	B	D	Y	W	M	K	Q	T	X

"Break a leg" Key

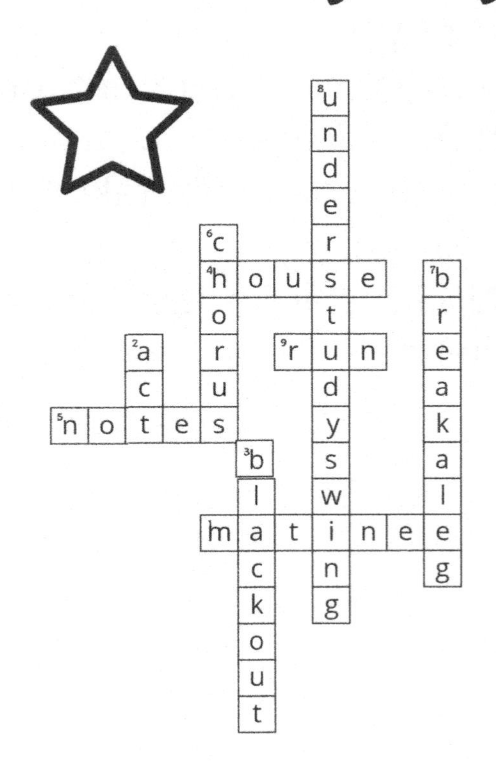

BRAVO! You finished DRAMA CLUB Activity Book & Glossary – Theater Edition!

As you continue your creative journey remember–
BE. DO. HAVE.
BE–I say I'm an actor.
DO– I'm creating & doing the play of an actor.
HAVE–I'm an actor.

Thanks so much for spending time with us and the DC gang.
Till next time, break a leg & stay curious!

More Actor Food?
Out now: A Life in the Theater: WORD SEARCH for Adults, Senior & Teens : Large Print
Coming soon : A Life in the Theater CROSSWORD for Adults, Seniors & Teens : Large Print
1000's of terms by theater profession and a walk through theater history.

Keep this book or purchase the keepsake, it will be a treasured item to look back on! To be notified of new Actor Food products, ACT Like a Business or Meal Prep: Actor Food for College & Young Professionals; click the QR#2.

1.VIDEO BONUS

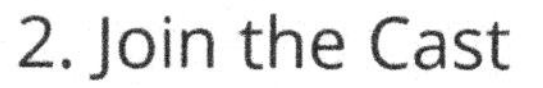

@ActorFood on Youtube/Subscribe/or follow us on Amazon
*Thank you for supporting the work & creativity of live human beings.

Made in the USA
Las Vegas, NV
11 January 2024